Written by Jean-Pierre Verdet
Illustrated by
Henri Galeron and Pierre-Marie Valat

*Specialist adviser: Dr Anita MacConnell,
Curator, Earth Sciences Collection,
The Science Museum, London*

*ISBN 1 85103 005 0
First published 1986 in the United Kingdom by
Moonlight Publishing Ltd.,
36 Stratford Road, London W8*

© *1985 by Editions Gallimard
Translated by Sarah Matthews
English text* © *1986 by Moonlight Publishing Ltd.
Printed in Italy by La Editoriale Libraria*

POCKET • WORLDS

The Air Around Us

The sky never stays the same...

THE WORLD OF NATURE

It is a really hot summer's day. The sky above you is a clear, unbroken blue – but look, towards the west, a few clouds are gathering. The very topmost branches of the trees begin to sway. The air is getting fresher and you can feel a wind starting to blow. The clouds thicken and gather across the sky. There's a storm on the way.

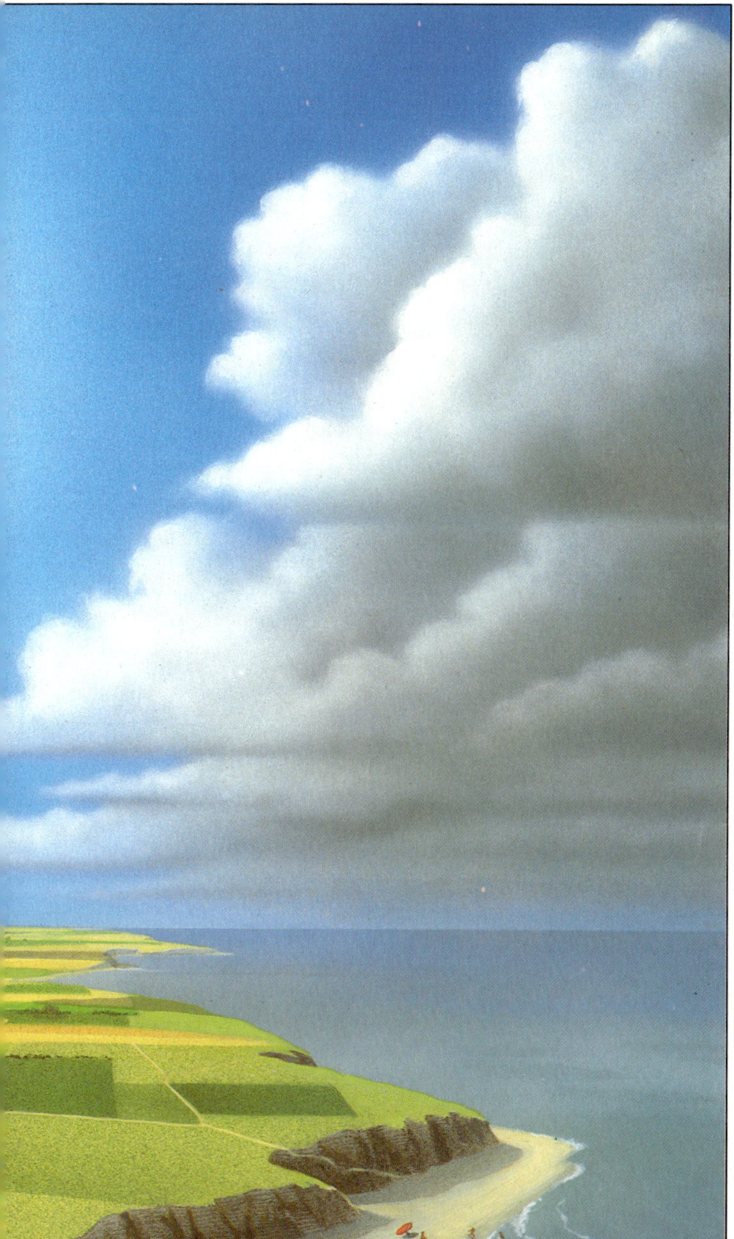

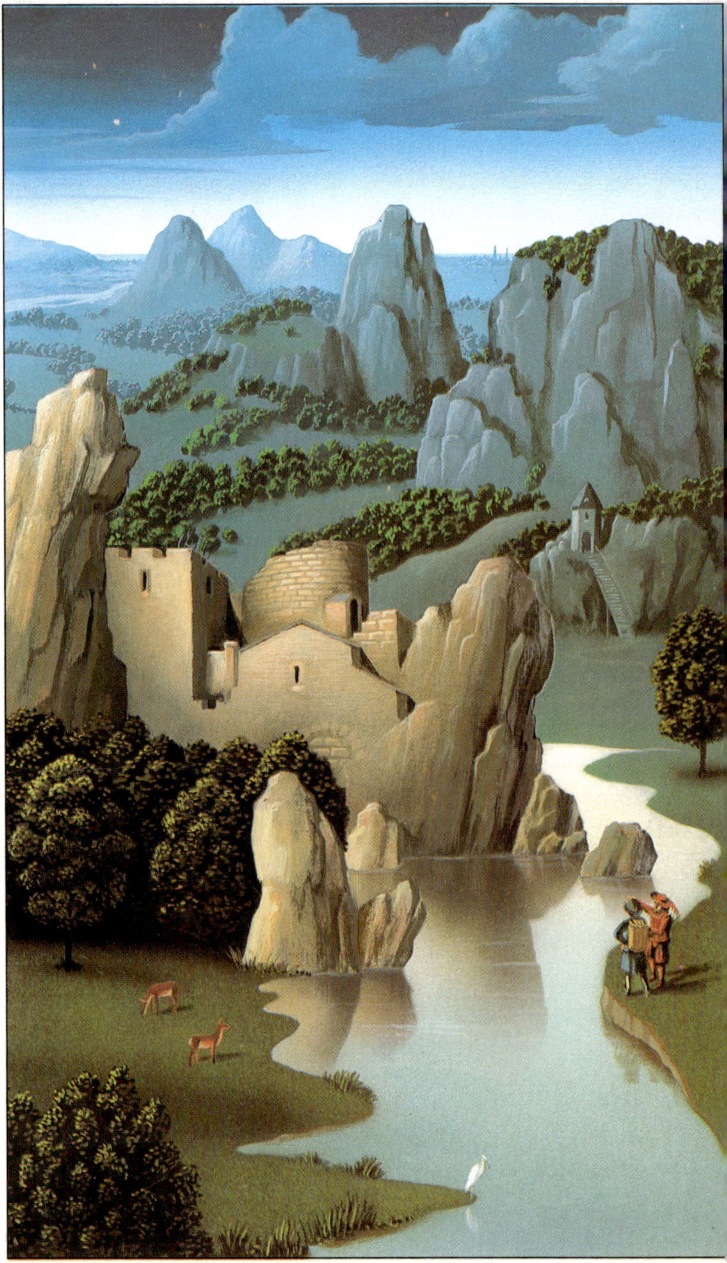

The air around us

It may seem as if the air is impossible to see and to feel, but in fact we see it and feel it all the time. In a small space like a room you can't see it, but outside, if you look into the distance, you can see the air far away as a misty blue. Painters, like the one who made this picture, love trying to copy the way in which things seem crisp and clear close to, but then become bluer and more hazy the further away they are.

What about feeling the air? Try holding your hand tightly over your nose and mouth. Almost immediately something happens – you go red! You start to choke! Quick, take a deep breath! There is oxygen in the air we breathe. Without it, even for a short time, we die.

Run very fast, with your arms and hands stretched out wide – can you feel the air pushing against you?

1. The sun is rising. This morning the air is damp, and sunbeams are reflected off the water in the air to make a white light.

3. On a fine day, as the sun rises, the air gets drier and clearer. The sky becomes a bright blue.

5. At sunset, the light shines red.

2. During the day, the sky changes colour.

4. It is the sunlight scattered by the gas and water in the air which gives the sky its different colours.

6. Once the sun has set, its rays no longer light up the air and the sky becomes dark.

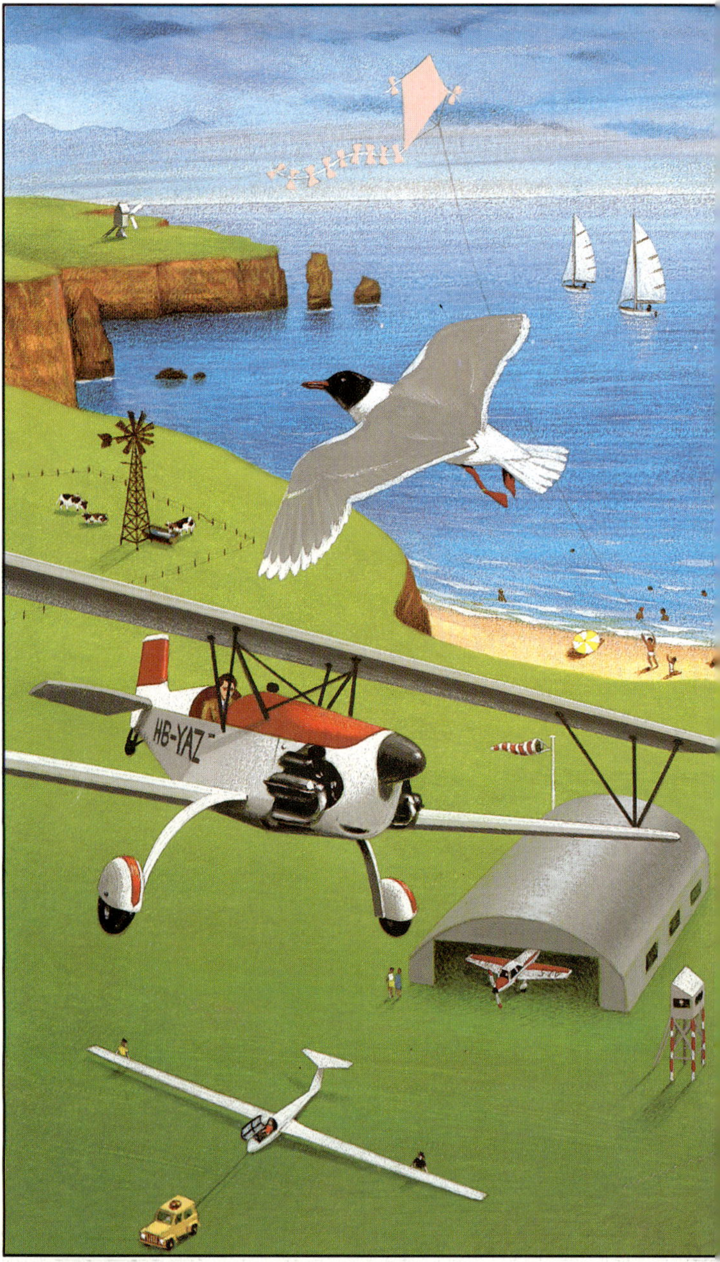
HB-YAZ

Weather satellite

The air is a mixture of gases. It is these gases which we breathe and which keep us alive. There is a layer of air wrapped round the earth, like the skin wrapped round an orange. We call this layer the **atmosphere.**

Clouds, rain, snow, hail, hurricanes, all grow in the part of the atmosphere that is closest to the earth. Weather satellites, orbiting the earth, take photographs of the atmosphere from space. These pictures help the weathermen to tell us what the weather is going to do next.

How can aeroplanes fly?

Planes, gliders, kites... and, of course, birds, are all held up by the air. Sailing boats are pushed along by the wind.

The earth and the main currents in the atmosphere as they appear from space

1. There is water in the air, in rivers, in the snow on top of mountains, but most of the water in the world is in the seas and oceans which cover over half its surface.

2. Round and round: rain falls and runs into the river, which flows into the sea. Water from the sea evaporates and rises into the air to make clouds. Clouds, pushed by the wind, travel over the land, where they break up as rain. Water is never lost!

3. Where do clouds come from?

The sun warms the water in the oceans and turns it into a fine, invisible vapour. The warm air, full of water vapour, rises until it meets colder air.

4. Cold air can hold less water vapour than warm air. As the air cools down, the vapour forms into droplets, like steam on a cold bathroom mirror. These droplets gather together to make clouds.

How can you tell which clouds are which?

There are lots of different types of clouds. **Stratus** clouds lie in thin layers, **cirrus** clouds are thin and feathery, **cumulus** are fat and fluffy. Clouds floating very high up, at over 6000 metres, start their names with cirro, while the lowest ones, that float at about 2000 metres, start with strato. The ones in between start with alto. High clouds are full of needles of ice, and are whiter than the grey, water-filled rain-clouds. **Cumulonimbus** clouds tower up through the sky: they are storm clouds.

1. Cirrus. 2. Alto-cumulus.
3. Cumulonimbus. 4. Cumulus.

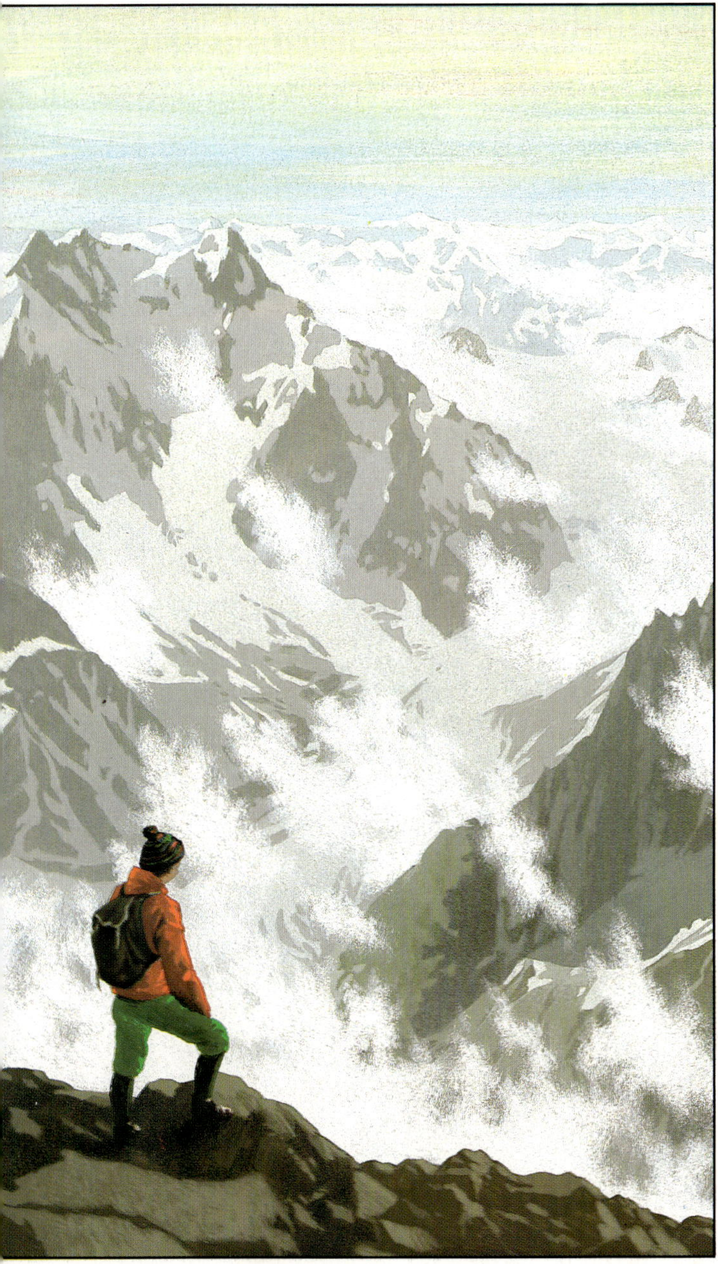

Where does rain come from?

Clouds are made of tiny drops of water, which join up to make bigger and bigger drops. When the drops are bigger than half a millimetre across, they get too heavy to stay up in the air. They fall out of the sky – as rain.

Earthworms, snails and slugs like to come out after the rain.

The weather in Europe is called 'temperate', half-way between the North Pole, where it is always cold and dry, and the Equator, where it is almost always hot and damp. In temperate countries, there are usually as many sunny days as rainy ones in a year.

There are some parts of the world, the **deserts**, where the ground is very warm. The air above is so hot that no clouds can form. This means that hardly any rain falls in the desert, and, without water, very few animals and plants can live there.

In the **tropics**, it rains a lot. Rain and sunshine follow each other in a regular pattern: first the wind blows off the sea, and it rains hard every day, then the wind blows from the land, and the weather is hot and dry.

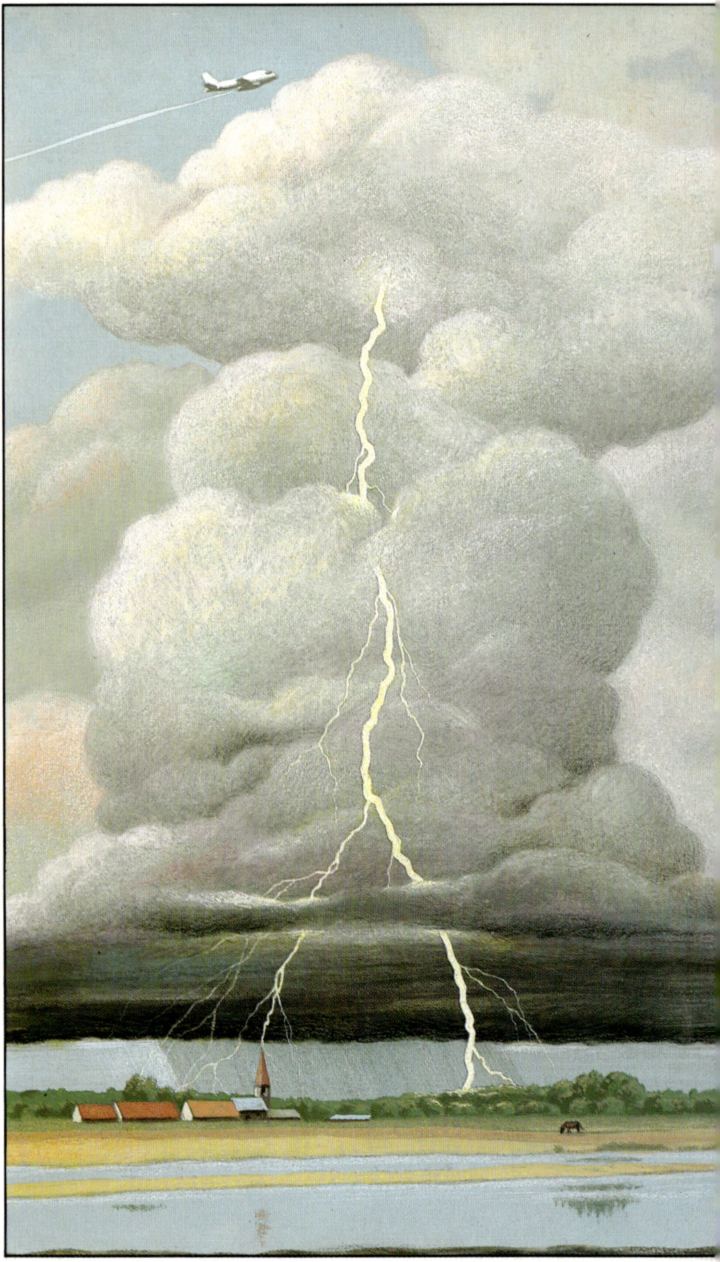

Big cumulonimbus clouds darken the sky: **a storm is coming.**

The wind gets stronger, and inside the clouds the water droplets are swirled up and down. This rush of movement creates electricity inside the clouds. Sparks leap out: lightning. The sound of thunder rolls across the sky. Big drops of rain start to fall. Quick, it's time to get home.

The Greek god Zeus throwing thunderbolts across the sky.

Lightning will often take the quickest way it can to reach the earth, running down anything high – a steeple, a tree, even an umbrella. Never shelter from a thunderstorm under a tree. Some buildings have lightning-conductors to lead the lightning safely to the ground.

Rainbows

Sunlight seems a clear, white light to us, but in fact it is made up of a whole number of different colours. When a ray of sunlight passes through a drop of water, the ray is very slightly bent. But every differently coloured ray is bent at a slightly different angle. That is why a drop of water can break up a sunbeam and make us see lots of different colours.

After a storm, the millions of drops of water hanging in the sky break up the light into a rainbow. In the sky, in the opposite direction to the sun, stands a semi-circle made up of every colour: red, orange, yellow, green, blue, indigo and violet. The colours are always in the same order. Try making your own rainbow by sprinkling a fine jet of water between yourself and the sun.

Snowflakes

If the air gets very cold very quickly, the clouds lose heat and the drops of water inside them turn to needles of ice. As they fall, these ice needles cling together and make starry snow crystals. These crystals, all caught up together, make snowflakes. Look at snowflakes under a magnifying glass or microscope, and see how each one makes a different pattern.

Sometimes, though, instead of turning to snow, the water droplets turn into hard round hailstones. Usually hailstones are small, and only sting you when they fall on you, but there have been hailstones as big as a pigeon's egg. Big hailstones can destroy whole fields of crops.

It can't hail or snow unless the weather is colder than 0 degrees centigrade. If it is any warmer than that, the water in the sky falls as rain.

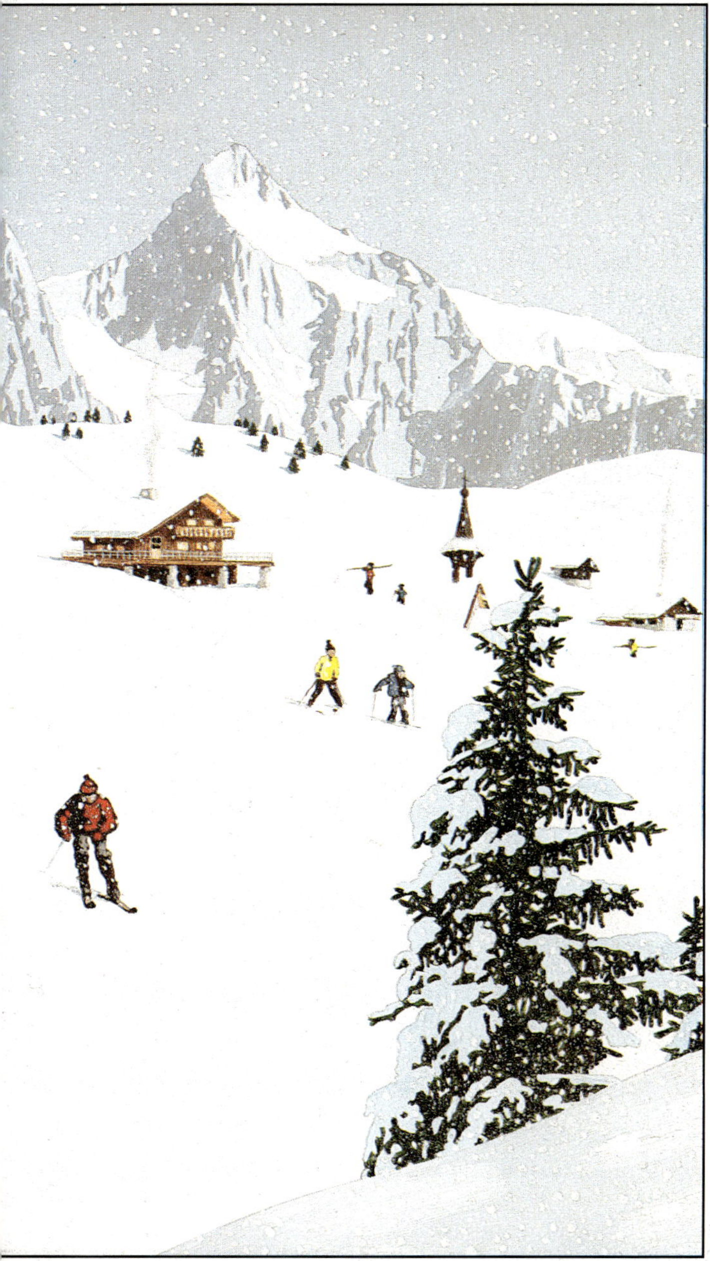

Force 0: calm

Force 3: gentle breeze

Force 6: brisk wind

Force 8: gusty wind

Force 10: storm

Force 12: hurricane

What is wind force?

The wind gets marks rather like your schoolwork, from 0 to 12 depending on its speed. Force 0 means no wind and force 12 means a hurricane, when the wind is travelling at over 120km an hour. The different numbers are called the Beaufort scale, after the English admiral who first thought of marking the wind-speed. Storms in Europe are usually around force 10. It is only in the tropics that you get force 12 hurricanes.

A whirlwind is a column of hot air which spins round as it rises and tears up everything in its path.

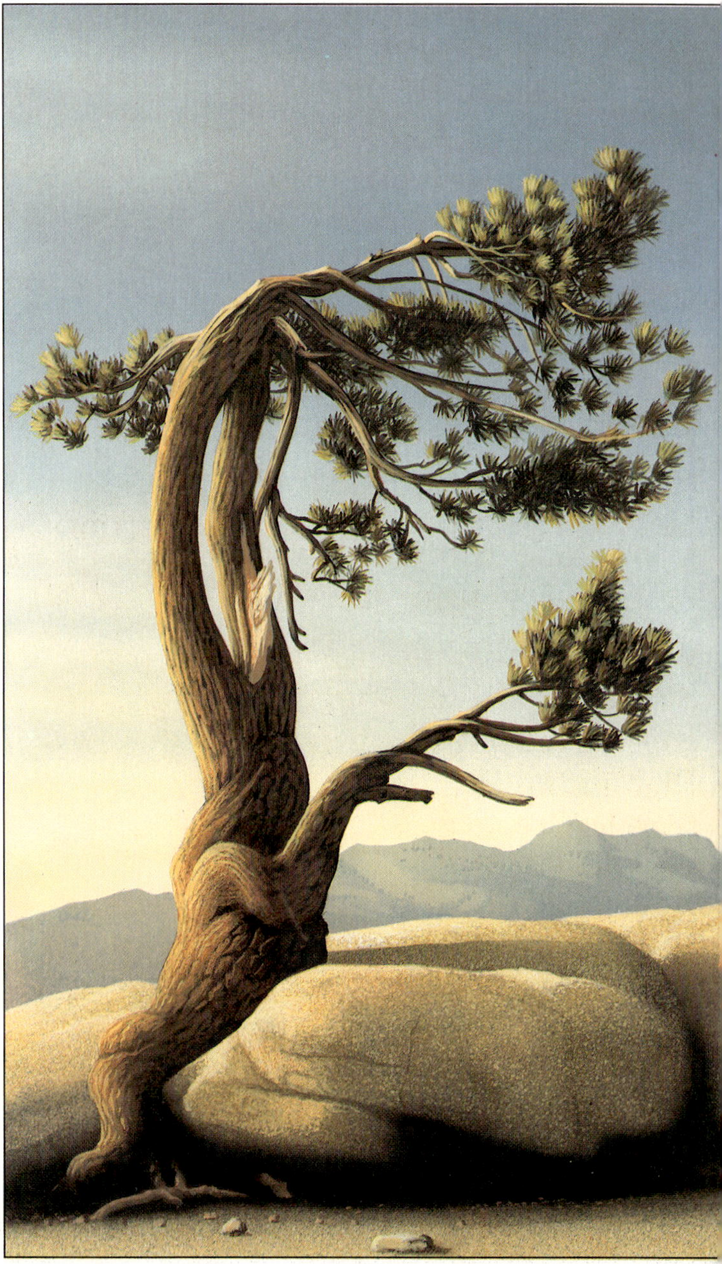

The wind is a big draught.

Warm air is lighter than cold air, and rises. It is the differences in heat between different parts of the air which create the wind. For instance, at the seaside, during the daytime, cold air rushes in off the sea and replaces the warm air over the beach – there is a sea-breeze. At night-time, the sea stays warmer than the land, and the breeze changes direction.

The wind carries seeds from place to place so that new plants can grow.

Sometimes there is no wind at ground level. Smoke from a chimney goes straight upwards. High in the sky, though, the clouds sail past – there is wind up there.

This windmill is making electricity, using the force of the wind as it turns the sails.

A tree which has been twisted by the wind

Spanish windmill   Dutch windmill   Greek windmill

There have been windmills in the world for a long time. They were one of man's earliest ideas for using the strength of nature to do his work for him. The sails of the windmill must face into the wind. As the wind pushes them round, they move machinery inside the mill. The movement can be used to grind corn, create electricity, draw up water… In pivot mills, only the roof is turned to face the sails into the wind, in a tower mill, the whole mill turns.

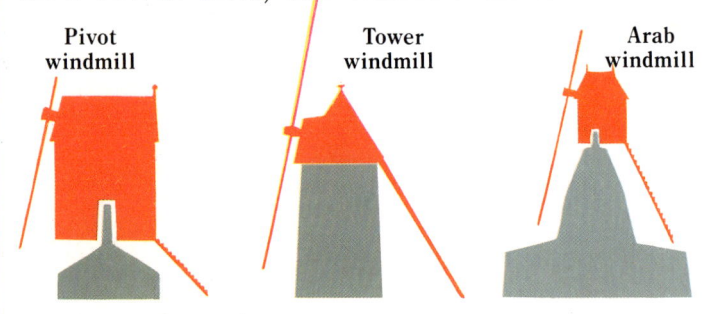

Pivot windmill   Tower windmill   Arab windmill

French windmill   Finnish windmill   Afghan windmill

Three ways of turning the mill to face the wind.

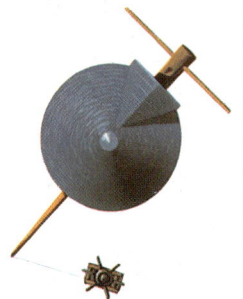

Human power   Animal power   Mechanical power

When the wind is too strong, it is a good idea to reduce the area of the sail.

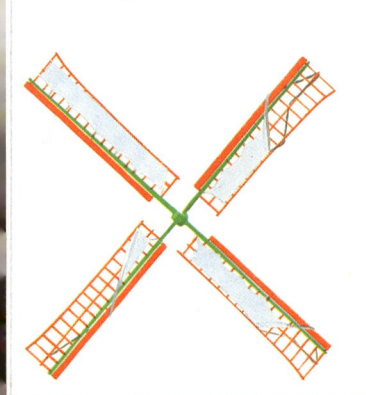

Cogwheels transmit the turning of the sails to the millstones.

Rings round the moon — rain's on the way.

If you watch the way clouds move, their colours, how strong the wind is blowing, and where it is coming from, you can often tell quite a lot about what the weather will do next. People who work the land, or who live in mountains, or sail the sea, use all sorts of signs to predict the weather.

Pine-cones,

for instance: they are very sensitive to dampness in the air. The scales on the cone close up when it is going to rain, and open out in dry weather.

When it is fine, I fling my windows wide. When cold weather comes, I close them again. What am I? A pine-cone.

The carline thistle

is a beautiful flower that looks like a little sun. In the South of France, they hang them over the doorway to predict the weather. The thistle opens up when the weather is turning fine, and shuts when the weather is nasty. In other parts of the world, other plants, and even seaweed are used in the same way.

The green frog

is one of the oldest weather forecasters in the world.

If you see a frog sitting out on a lawn or field, it means the air is nice and damp for him, and it will soon rain. If he hides away under a stone, then the air is dry and sunshine is on the way.

You can predict the weather with the branch of pine-tree which has a twig forking off it. Strip off the bark and nail it to a plank. If the weather is damp, the twig will stand up; if it is very dry, it will lie down.

This balloon is carrying measuring instruments up into the atmosphere.

What will the weather be like tomorrow?

These days, weathermen use lots of different scientific instruments for measuring the speed and direction of the wind, the temperature and dampness of the air and the pressure, which means the weight of the atmosphere.

There are weather stations placed all round the earth, on land and on special ships which criss-cross the oceans.

Measuring instruments high in the sky help predict the weather.

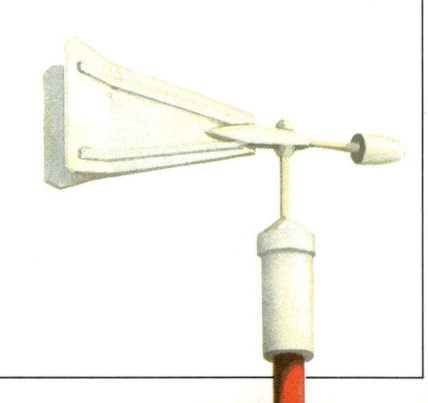

The weather–vane shows the direction of the wind.

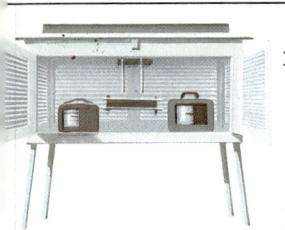

A thermometer screen

Inside the thermometer measures how hot the air is, a hygrometer measures how damp it is, and a barograph measures the pressure.

A barometer measures the pressure of the atmosphere. The layer of air above us weighs about a kilogram per square centimetre. If the pressure is low, the weather will be bad, if it is high, it will be changeable.

A barograph

An anemometer measures the speed of the wind. The harder the wind blows, the faster the anemometer turns round. You will see them on the top of cranes, or on airport buildings Some jobs are dangerous when the wind is blowing too hard.

Pocket Worlds – building up into a child's first encyclopaedia:

<u>The Natural World</u>
The Air Around Us
The Sunshine Around Us
The Moon and Stars Around Us
Our Blue Planet
Coast and Seashore
Mountains of the World
Volcanoes of the World
Deserts and Jungles
Rocks and Stones
In the Hedgerow
The Life of the Tree
Woodland and Forest
The Pond
Fruits of the Earth

<u>The Animal World</u>
Prehistoric Animals
The Long Life and Gentle Ways of the Elephant
Big Bears and Little Bears
Big Cats and Little Cats
Farm Animals Around the World
Cows and Their Cousins
All About Pigs
The Horse
Monkeys and Apes
Crocodiles and Alligators
Whales, Dolphins and Seals
Wolf!
Bees, Ants and Termites
Caterpillars, Butterflies and Moths
Birds and Their Nests
Wildlife Alert!
Wildlife in Towns
Animals in Winter
Animals on the Move
Animals Underground
Animal Architects
Animal Colours and Patterns
Teeth and Fangs

<u>The World of Food</u>
Chocolate, Tea and Coffee
Bread Around the World

The Potato
The Story of a Grain of Rice
Milk
All About Salt
All About Sugar

The World We Use
All About Wool
The Wonderful Story of Silk
The Story of Paper
What Is Glass?
From Oil to Plastic
Metals and Their Secrets
Energy

The Human World
Living in Ancient Egypt
Living in Ancient Greece
Living in Ancient Rome
Living with the Eskimos
Living in the Sahara
Living in India
Living on a Tropical Island
Living in Australia

Living in the Heart of Africa
On the Trail of the American Indians
Cowboys and Pioneers
The Building of the Great Cathedrals
Long Ago in a Castle
The Other Side of the Screen
Firemen to the Rescue
The Making of Music
The Story of Writing
People Who Work While We Sleep
Bridges, Tunnels and Towers
Transport Yesterday and Today
The Long and Rich History of Trade
Money Through the Ages
Measuring the World
Sleep and Dreams
Your Body
The Five Senses
The Story of Birth and Babies